FORTY MARTYRS
OF ENGLAND AND WALES

Canonised by His Holiness Pope Paul VI
on 25 October 1970

Compiled by
James Walsh, SJ
Vice-Postulator for the Cause of the English Martyrs

CATHOLIC TRUTH SOCIETY
PUBLISHERS TO THE HOLY SEE

Contents

INTRODUCTION

To Bear Witness to the Truth

From the Catechism of the Catholic Church

Before Pilate, Christ proclaims that he 'has come into the world, to bear witness to the truth'. The Christian is not to 'be ashamed then of testifying to our Lord'. In situations that require witness to the faith, the Christian must profess it without equivocation, after the example of St Paul before his judges. We must keep 'a clear conscience towards God and towards men'.

The duty of Christians to take part in the life of the Church impels them to act as witnesses of the Gospel and of the obligations that flow from it. This witness is a transmission of the faith in words and deeds. Witness is an act of justice that establishes the truth or makes it known.

All Christians by the example of their lives and the witness of their word, wherever they live, have an obligation to manifest the new man which they have put on in Baptism, and to reveal the power of the Holy Spirit by whom they were strengthened at Confirmation.

Martyrdom is the supreme witness given to the truth of the faith: it means bearing witness even unto death. The martyr bears witness to Christ who died and rose, to whom he is united by charity. He bears witness to the truth of the faith and of Christian doctrine. He endures death through an act of fortitude. 'Let me become the food of the beasts, through whom it will be given me to reach God.'

The Church has painstakingly collected the records of those who persevered to the end in witnessing to their faith. These are the acts of the martyrs. They form the archives of truth written in letters of blood:

Neither the pleasures of the world nor the kingdoms of this age will be of any use to me. It is better for me to die [in order to unite myself] to Christ Jesus than to reign over the ends of the earth. I seek him who died for us; I desire him who rose for us. My birth is approaching...

(St Ignatius of Antioch)

I bless you for having judged me worthy from this day and this hour to be counted among your martyrs... You have kept your promise, God of faithfulness and truth. For this reason and for everything, I praise you, I bless you, I glorify you through the eternal and heavenly High Priest, Jesus Christ, your beloved Son. Through him, who is with you and the Holy Spirit, may glory be given to you, now and in the ages to come. Amen.

(Martyrdom of Polycarp)

Why were they executed?

The following were the Acts under which the martyrs were charged:

The Treason Act of 1352 (Edward III, stat.5, cap.2). This is still the basic treason law of England. It defined treason as compassing or attempting the death of the king or his heirs.

An Act to retain the Queen's Majesty's subjects in due obedience (23 Eliz.I, cap.1, 1581). This Act made it high treason to reconcile or be reconciled to the Catholic Church or to induce others to be so reconciled ('persuading to popery'). It covered 'seditious words against the Queen'.

An Act against Jesuits, seminary priests and such other like disobedient persons (27 Eliz.I, cap.2, 1585). This Act made it high treason for a Catholic priest ordained abroad to come into or remain in the realm after 24 June 1559. It made it felony for anyone to harbour or assist him. The sentence for a priest was that he should be hanged, drawn and quartered, for a layman, that he be hanged. Sometimes secondary charges were added.

Will Christians of other Churches be offended?

During the preparation of the Cause of the Eighty-five Martyrs *(CTS: H 481)* the ecumenical implications had always been borne in mind. Care has been taken at all stages to present the Cause in such a way that the happy relations existing between the Churches should not be damaged. The outcome of the Cause was most generously received on all sides. Before the canonisation of the Forty Martyrs in 1970 the British Council of Churches declared: '... the martyr tradition is one in which all have shared and from which all may draw strength, even across denominational boundaries'. In a statement released when the beatification of the Eighty-five Martyrs was announced, his Grace the Archbishop of Canterbury said: 'I warmly welcome the irenical and ecumenical manner in which Cardinal Basil Hume has announced his Holiness Pope John Paul II's intention to beatify a further eight-five Roman Catholic martyrs from England, Scotland and Wales... With Cardinal Hume I hope that the beatification of the Eighty-five Martyrs will indeed prompt all the Christians of England, Wales and Scotland to pursue the path of reconciliation and reunion with greater understanding and effectiveness'. This beatification took place on 22nd November 1987, the day of their memorial.

May the blood of the Martyrs, and their prayers, indeed assist in healing the wounds caused by our divisions!

SAINT JOHN HOUGHTON, SAINT ROBERT LAWRENCE, AND SAINT AUGUSTINE WEBSTER

These three Carthusian Priors, were martyred together on 4 May 1535. They were the first martyrs of the English Reformation. John Houghton came from Essex and had studied at the University of Cambridge. He joined the London Charterhouse about 1515, was elected Prior of Beauvale in Nottinghamshire in 1531, and later the same year became Prior of London. Robert Lawrence was a monk of the London Charterhouse who had succeeded John Houghton as Prior of Beauvale. Augustine Webster, a monk of Sheen Charterhouse, near London, and also a graduate of Cambridge, had been Prior of Axholme in Lincolnshire since 1531. After the Act of Supremacy of 1534, which declared King Henry VIII to be supreme head of the Church in England, Lawrence and Webster came to London to consult with John Houghton about the religious issues involved. The three Priors approached Thomas Cromwell, the King's chief minister, and tried to get for their communities a form of the oath of supremacy that would be acceptable in conscience, but they failed and were committed to the Tower of London. At their trial they pleaded not guilty of the treason with which they were charged and firmly maintained that the King could not be head of the Church. The jury deliberated at length without result, but were finally coerced by Cromwell's threats into bringing in a verdict of guilty. On the last day of their lives St Thomas More, from his prison window in the Tower, saw the martyrs being taken out to Tyburn, and, turning to his daughter, said: 'Lo, dost thou not see, Meg, that these blessed fathers be now as cheerfully going to their deaths as bridegrooms to their marriage?' Many of the Court are said to have been present as the monks were hanged, drawn and quartered. All three refused the pardon offered them at the last moment if they would accept the King's supremacy.

Saint Richard Reynolds

Perhaps the most learned monk of his time and certainly one of the holiest. He joined the Bridgettine Order at Syon Abbey, Isleworth, on the outskirts of London, in 1513, after a distinguished career at Cambridge, where he had been a Fellow of Corpus Christi College. It was thought that if such a learned and saintly man were to accept the King as head of the Church, this would put many consciences at rest. He was therefore tendered the oath of supremacy, but he absolutely refused to take it. As a result he was tried with the three Carthusian Priors and hanged, drawn and quartered with them at Tyburn on 4 May 1535. The last of the four to suffer, he encouraged his fellow martyrs with the promise of 'a heavenly banquet and supper for their sharp breakfast, taken patiently for their Master's sake'. Like them, he also refused the pardon offered for a last-minute acknowledgment of the King's supremacy.

Saint John Stone

He was an Augustinian Friar (Austin Friar) belonging to the Canterbury house of that order. We know little of his early life. In 1538 Henry VIII had started on the dissolution of the monasteries and on Saturday 14 December 1538 Richard Ingworth, an apostate Dominican, and at that time Bishop of Dover, called on the Friary to close it down. Every friar had to sign a formal document explicitly acknowledging Henry VIII as head of the Church in England. John Stone refused to sign. Ingworth described the meeting in a letter to Chancellor Cromwell:

'Being in the austin friars there the 14th day of December, one Friar there very rudely and traitorously used him(self) before all the company as by a bill here inclosed you shall perceive part. To write half his words and order there it were too long to write. I perceiving his demeanour straight sequestered him so that none spoke with him. I sent for the mayor and ere that he came I examined him before master Spilman and also afterwards before the mayor and master Spilman and at all times he still held and still will to die for it that the King may not be head of the Church of England, but it must be a spiritual father appointed by God.'

John Stone was sent to London and was left in the Tower for many months. However on 27 October 1539 a commission of 'Oyer et Terminer' (Hear and Determine) was addressed to the Mayor of Canterbury and four other worthy gentlemen of that town. So Friar Stone was sent back to Canterbury to be tried for treason under the 1535 Treason Act, which declared that the penalty for High Treason was to be executed on anyone who might 'maliciously desire to deprive the King of his title of Supreme Head of the Church'. There was no appeal allowed.

While awaiting trial at Canterbury, Friar Stone would have been kept in the cells at Canterbury Castle. His friend Nicolas Harpsfield relates the following details:

'Having poured forth prayers in prison to God and fasted continuously for three days, he heard a voice though he saw no one, which addressed him by name and bade him to be of good heart and not to hesitate to suffer death with constancy for the belief which he had professed. From which afterwards he gained such eagerness and strength as never to allow himself by persuasion or terror to be drawn from his purpose.'

We do not know the exact date of his trial in December 1539. It seems likely that the execution took place on December 27. His last days would have been spent in the Westgate Prison. In order to show the populace that John Stone was an exceptional criminal the actual execution took place on the Donjean (now called Dane John), a prominent hillock by the city walls and overlooking the by then empty friary. Here John Stone was hanged, drawn and quartered. We have no record of his last words but we do have the bill of expenses for the execution. The total cost came to sixteen shillings and one penny. This included the hangman's fee, the cost of the wood, and even small items like the cost of a drink for those who set up the gallows.

The modern pilgrim can climb to the top of the Dane John today and visualise the gallows standing where the war memorial stands now.

Saint Cuthbert Mayne

The protomartyr of the English seminaries, came from the West Country. Born near Barnstaple in Devon, he studied at the University of Oxford, where he took orders in the Church of England and became chaplain at St John's College. Under the influence of Catholic friends, among whom was St Edmund Campion, Mayne became uneasy about his religious position. He left Oxford, was reconciled to the Catholic Church, and eventually entered the newly established English College at Douai, where he was ordained priest in 1575. At his own earnest request he returned to England the following year and began to work in Cornwall. He took up residence at the manor house of Francis Tregian in that county, where his work as steward of the Tregian estates was for a time an effective disguise for his priestly ministry. He was taken, however, a year later and condemned to death at Launceston Assizes, on a trumped-up charge of bringing into the country and promulgating a papal bull. He was hanged, drawn and quartered at Launceston on 30 November 1577.

Saint Edmund Campion

He was born in London about 1540. He studied in his native city and then at the University of Oxford, where he became a Fellow of St John's College. He took deacon's orders in the Protestant Church about 1566, but, gradually becoming more and more dissatisfied with the new religion, he left Oxford in 1570. After spending some time in Ireland, he crossed to the Continent and entered the English College at Douai. In 1573 he joined the Society of Jesus in Rome. Ordained priest in Prague in 1578, he and Fr Robert Persons were chosen as the first two Jesuits to be sent on the English mission. Campion landed at Dover in June 1580 and during the next year worked in various parts of England, using the disguise of a fashionable gentleman. He also published, from a secret printing press at Stonor Park, near Henley-on-Thames, his *Decem Rationes* – ten reasons demonstrating the truth of the Catholic religion. Three weeks later he was captured at

Lyford in Berkshire and brought to London. Imprisoned in the Tower of London and severely tortured, he could still more than hold his own in disputation with Protestant adversaries, against whom he argued with spirit. Tried with St Ralph Sherwin and St Luke Kirby on a false charge of plotting against Queen Elizabeth I, he put up a brilliant defence, but the rigged jury brought in a verdict of guilty. Before the sentence was pronounced Campion addressed the court, saying: 'In condemning us you condemn all your own ancestors… God lives. Posterity will live. Their judgment is not so liable to corruption as that of those who now sentence us to death.' He was offered every kind of inducement to bring him to conform, but, constant to the end, he was hanged, drawn and quartered at Tyburn on 1 December 1581.

Saint Ralph Sherwin

The protomartyr of the English College, Rome, was born at Rodsley, Derbyshire. He conformed to the new religion, but was reconciled to the Catholic Church during his student days at Exeter College, Oxford. In 1575 he went overseas to the seminary at Douai, and two years later was ordained priest there. He continued his studies at the English college in Rome, where his name stands first in the College register. When the students of the College were required to affirm on oath their readiness to be sent on the English mission, he did so and added:

'Today rather than tomorrow'. He returned to England in 1580 but was soon arrested and imprisoned in the Marshalsea and afterwards in the Tower of London, where he was put in irons and tortured. These irons he called his 'little bells', and remarked: 'I have never heard such sweet harmony before'. They racked him and exposed him in the snow alternately. Once the racking lasted for five days and nights, and all the time he was kept without food or drink, but he never spoke. He was promised the second bishopric of England if he would conform. To his uncle he wrote: 'Innocency is my only comfort against all the forged villainy which is fathered on my fellow priests and me'. And to some friends: 'I appeal to my Redeemer's clemency. I have no boldness but in his blood. His bitter Passion is my only consolation.' He was hanged, drawn and quartered, with St Edmund Campion and St Alexander Briant, at Tyburn on 1 December 1581.

Saint Alexander Briant

From Somerset, he studied at Hart Hall, Oxford, and at Douai, where he was ordained priest in 1578. The following year he returned to Somerset as a missionary. In 1581 he was arrested in London, in a house adjoining that used by Fr Robert Persons. His captors were disappointed that they failed to apprehend Persons, but they were sure that Briant knew his whereabouts and determined to wring the information from him. For two days he was deprived of food and drink, and when this brought no result he was moved to the Tower of London, where he was racked severely. His persecutors then thrust needles under his nails, but he still refused to give any information. After this he was cast for eight days into a pit twenty feet deep and without light. Then he was brought back to the torture chamber again and racked on two successive days, until his body was disjointed. In all these sufferings he never revealed a single secret. Thomas Norton, the torturer in the Tower, admitted that the martyr was entirely unmoved by threats to 'make him a foot longer than God had made him'. During his torture he promised God that he would seek admission to the Society of Jesus. He did so and was accepted before his death. He was hanged, drawn and quartered at Tyburn, after St Edmund Campion and St Ralph Sherwin, on 1 December 1581.

Saint John Paine

Saint John Paine was born at Peterborough in Northamptonshire. He entered the English College at Douai in 1574 and was ordained priest there in 1576. Returning to England with St Cuthbert Mayne the same year, he worked chiefly in Essex, making Ingatestone Hall, the home of Lady Ann Petre (widow of Sir William Petre) his headquarters. A notorious spy, George Eliot, betrayed him, and after two severe rackings in the Tower he was tried. He received his sentence calmly, saying: 'If it please the Queen and her Council that I shall die, I refer my cause to God'. After refusing a pardon on condition that he would conform, he was hanged, drawn and quartered at Chelmsford on 2 April 1582.

Saint Luke Kirby

Someone who never quite lost his schoolboy sense of adventure. Travelling through Switzerland with St Edmund Campion and St Ralph Sherwin, he challenged Theodore Beza, the great Calvinist, to a dispute, on the condition that the loser should suffer death. When a student in Rome, acting on impulse, he gave the shirt he was wearing to a beggar. He was a Yorkshireman and a university graduate, probably of Cambridge. In 1576 he entered the English College at Douai, and after ordination there finished his studies in Rome. He was captured immediately on arrival in England. As a prisoner in the Gatehouse and later in the Tower of London, he showed the steadfastness of his character. That ingenious instrument of torture, the 'Scavenger's Daughter' (so named after its inventor, Sir William Skevington), was used on him, but with no effect, and on 30 May 1582 he was hanged, drawn and quartered at Tyburn.

Saint Richard Gwyn

The first Welsh martyr of Elizabeth I's reign, was born about 1537 in Llanidloes, Montgomeryshire. He studied for a short time at Oxford, and then went to St John's College, Cambridge. Returning to Wales abut 1562, he became a schoolmaster and taught in Flintshire and Denbighshire.

Richard Gwyn was married and had six children. Arrested in Wrexham in 1578, he escaped, but he was arrested again in 1580. After being tried and remanded several times at the Assizes, he was finally condemned to death at Wrexham, in October 1584, for refusing to recognise the Queen as head of the Church in England and persuading others to become Catholics. Two days before his death he was offered his freedom if he would conform to the State religion. As Gwyn left the prison on his way to execution, he said to his fellow prisoners: 'Weep not for me, for I do but pay the rent before the rent day'. On the scaffold he forgave his executioner, acknowledged Elizabeth I to be the lawful Queen of England and denied that he had ever committed any treason against her; but he still refused to recognise her as head of the Church. As he prayed 'O God, be merciful to me a sinner', he was turned off the ladder and cut down while still alive and disembowelled. He suffered at Wrexham on 15 October 1584.

Saint Margaret Clitherow

She was a butcher's wife in York. Her husband, John, once a Catholic, had conformed to the new religion, in which she herself also had been brought up. In 1574, three years after their marriage, Margaret was reconciled to the Catholic Church and became a zealous helper of the Catholic cause. Priests were constantly harboured in her house, and she kept a Catholic schoolmaster for her own children and those of a few neighbours. During twelve years of such apostolic activity she spent a total of nearly three years in prison. Eventually the Sheriff's men searched her house and threatened one of the pupils attending her school until he revealed to them the priest's hiding place and the Mass vestments. When brought before the Judge, Margaret refused to plead, in order to save the conscience of the jury and spare her children and servants the ordeal of giving evidence against her. As a result the Judge was obliged to pass the barbaric sentence required by the law in such cases: 'You must be stripped naked, laid down, your back upon the ground, and as much weight laid on you as you are able to bear, and so continue three days without meat or drink, except a little barley bread and puddle water, and the third day be pressed to death, your hands and feet tied to posts and a sharp stone under you back'. The three-day sentence was not carried out, but on 25 March 1586 she was crushed to death, in the Tollbooth, on Ouse Bridge, in York. She took a quarter of an hour to die. Her husband never returned to the Catholic faith, but a daughter of hers afterwards became a nun at Louvain.

Saint Margaret Ward

Margaret came from Congleton, Cheshire, When she heard that there was a neglected priest, Fr William Watson, in the Bridewell prison in London, she resolved to visit him. By making friends with the gaoler's wife she got permission to see him. At first she was thoroughly searched before and after her visits, but gradually the authorities became less strict and she was able to smuggle in a rope. Fr Watson made his escape, but in the confusion he left behind the incriminating rope. The gaoler immediately guessed that Margaret was responsible and had her arrested. She was kept in irons for eight days and was hung up by her hands and scourged. At her trial she readily admitted that she had helped Fr Watson to escape and absolutely refused to disclose his whereabouts. She was offered a pardon on condition that she attended the Protestant church services, but she would not do so. She was hanged at Tyburn on 30 August 1588.

Saint Edmund Gennings

Born in Lichfield, Staffordshire, in 1567, he was brought up a Protestant. At the age of sixteen he became a page to a Catholic gentleman, Richard Sherwood. Impressed by his master's example, Edmund asked to be received into the Catholic Church. When Mr Sherwood left England to become a priest, Edmund followed. He was not of a very robust constitution, and in the English College at Rheims he was found to be suffering from tuberculosis. After some time spent at Le Havre he recovered, miraculously it was believed, and resumed his studies at Rheims. He was ordained in 1590, by special dispensation as he was still under the canonical age, and then returned to England, landing at Whitby in Yorkshire. Within a year, however, his mission came to an end. He was saying Mass in the house of St Swithun Wells in London, when Richard Topcliffe, the well-known persecutor of Catholics, with his officers, burst in. The congregation decided to oppose force with force rather than allow a sacrilege. They held the door and beat back the invaders until the Mass was finished, when they surrendered quietly. Edmund Gennings was hanged, drawn and quartered outside Swithun Wells's house on 10 December 1591. His brother, John, who up to this time had been a Protestant, was converted by Edmund's martyrdom. He went to Douai, became a priest and later a Franciscan, and wrote Edmund's biography. Many miracles are said to have been worked through the intercession of St Edmund Gennings.

Saint Swithun Wells

He came from Brambridge in Hampshire, and for many years was a schoolmaster at Monkton Farleigh in

Wiltshire. During this period he attended Protestant services, but in 1583 he was reconciled to the Catholic
Church. Two years later he moved to London, taking a
house in Gray's Inn Fields. In 1591 St Edmund Gennings
and St Polydore Plasden were arrested in this house when
it was raided during Fr Gennings's Mass. Swithun Wells
himself was absent at the time, but on his return he was
immediately imprisoned. At his trial he said he had not
been present at the Mass but wished he had been, to
which the Judge said that 'though he was not at the feast,
he should taste of the sauce'. His wife, Alice, was also
condemned but to her great sorrow reprieved; she died in
prison ten years later. On his way to execution the martyr
caught sight of an old hunting companion, whom he
greeted with the words: 'Farewell, dear friend! Farewell
all hawking, hunting and old pastimes; I am now going a
better way.' On the scaffold he said to Richard Topcliffe:
'I pray God make you of a Saul a Paul, of a bloody persecutor one of the Catholic Church's children'. He was
hanged on 10 December 1591, outside his own house,
where St Edmund Gennings suffered with him.

Saint Eustace White

He was born at Louth in Lincolnshire. His father, an
ardent Protestant, solemnly cursed him when he was converted to the Catholic faith. He was ordained priest in
Rome in 1588, and then returned to England and worked

in the West Country for three years. Arrested in Dorset, he was brought to London and imprisoned in the Bridewell prison. He was tortured several times by Richard Topcliffe, and once was hung up by his hands for eight hours on end. Yet in all his agony they could never extract a word from him except his prayer: 'Lord, more pain if thou pleasest, and more patience'. He was condemned to death for his priesthood and hanged, drawn and quartered at Tyburn, with St Polydore Plasden, on 10 December 1591.

Saint Polydore Plasden

His real name was Oliver Palmer, and he was born at Fleet Bridge (near the present Ludgate Circus) in London. He studied at Rheims and Rome, where he was ordained priest, and returned to England to work in his native London. He was arrested with St Edmund Gennings and condemned to death as a priest. Sir Walter Raleigh was present at his execution, and hearing him pray for the Queen, asked, 'What dost thou think as thou prayest?' After further questions Raleigh realised that here was no traitor. He ordered the execution to be postponed until he went to plead with the Queen. But Richard Topcliffe intervened, and put to Plasden what was known as 'the bloody question': 'Then thou thinkest not to defend the Queen against the Pope, if he could come to establish thy religion?' Plasden answered: 'I am a Catholic priest, therefore I would never fight, nor counsel others to fight, against my religion, for that were to deny my faith'. And kissing the rope, he went on: 'O Christ, I will never deny thee for a thousand lives'. After this avowal Sir Walter allowed the execution to proceed, but he insisted that Plasden be allowed to die before he was cut down. He was hanged, drawn and quartered at Tyburn on 10 December 1591.

Saint John Boste

Born at Dufton, near Appleby in Westmorland, about 1543, though others think it was 1550. He was elected MA and Fellow of Queen's College, Oxford, in 1572, and in 1574 became Master of Appleby Grammar School. In 1576 he was received into the Church at Brome in Suffolk. In 1578 he returned to Oxford and was re-elected Fellow. Shortly afterwards he was expelled on religious grounds. He crossed over to France, studied for the priesthood at Rheims and was ordained on 4 March 1581. Returning to England, he ministered for a time in Norfolk and then came North where he was to spend the rest of his priestly life. He was described by Huntingdon, Lord President of the North, as 'the greatest stag in the North', and every effort was made to capture him. Through the treachery of an apostate Catholic, Francis Eglesfield, he was betrayed at the Waterhouse, some four miles from Durham, just after he had said Mass. He was imprisoned first at Durham and then taken to London where he was confined in the Tower. Here he was cruelly racked and permanently crippled. He was brought back to Durham to stand his trial. This took place on 24 July 1594 and he was executed the same day. As he climbed the ladder to the gallows, he recited the Rosary and died asking God's forgiveness for his executioner.

Saint Robert Southwell

Born at Horsham St Faith, Norfolk, in 1562. His father, a courtier of Elizabeth I, conformed to Protestantism out of ambition. His mother, however, remained a Catholic and Robert was brought up in the old faith. He was only in his fifteenth year when he entered the English College at Douai, and two years later he sought admission to the Society of Jesus in Belgium but was refused on account of his youth. He persisted, however, and showed his determination by walking all the way to Rome, where he was admitted to the Jesuit novitiate in 1578. Ordained priest, he returned to England in 1586 and for the next six years he laboured with great zeal and success in and around London. It was at this time also that he produced his many well-known works of prose and poetry, which give him an honoured place in the history of the golden age of English literature. He had many hairbreadth escapes, but was finally arrested near Harrow in 1592, betrayed by a Catholic girl who had fallen into the hands of Richard Topcliffe. He was tortured with extreme severity both in Topcliffe's house and in the Tower of London, but his tormentors failed completely to extract any confessions from him. After two and a half years in prison he was tried in Westminster Hall and condemned to death for his priesthood. Next day, 21 February 1595, at the age of thirty-three, he was hanged, drawn and quartered at Tyburn. On the scaffold he prayed for the Queen, professed his faith and his priesthood, and begged his friends to pray for his perseverance in the final struggle. His last words were: 'This my death, my last farewell to this unfortunate life, and yet to me most happy and most fortunate. I pray it may be for the full satisfaction of my sins, for the good of my country, and for the comfort of many others. Which death, although it seems here disgraceful, yet I hope that in time to come it will be to my eternal glory.'

Saint Henry Walpole

From Docking, Norfolk, he studied at the grammar school in Norwich, Peterhouse in Cambridge, Gray's Inn in London, and at Rheims and Rome. He entered the Society of Jesus in Rome in 1584 and was ordained priest in Paris in 1588. The following year, while acting as chaplain with the Spanish forces in the Netherlands, he was captured by the English and imprisoned at Flushing. Released in January 1590, he longed to work in England, but for some time permission was withheld and he was sent to teach in English seminaries in Spain and Flanders. Haunted by the example of his fellow Jesuit, Fr John Gerard, he often remarked: 'Gerard doth much good. Why not I?' On 4 December 1593 he landed at Flamborough Head, Yorkshire. Twenty-four hours later he was arrested and imprisoned, first at York and then in the Tower of London. In the Tower he was tortured severely, in a vain effort to extract from him information about Catholics he had known in England and abroad. Finally he was sent back to York for his trial. He was offered life and liberty if he would abjure the Pope and admit the spiritual supremacy of the Queen, but he refused. He was hanged, drawn and quartered at York on 7 April 1595.

Saint Philip Howard

Born in London, at Arundel House, on 28 June 1557, the son of that Thomas, Duke of Norfolk, whom Elizabeth executed in 1572 for his share in the plot to enthrone Mary, Queen of Scots; the Duke's father was the famous poet, Henry, Earl of Surrey, executed by Henry VIII in 1547.

Earl Philip had a royal godfather in the person of Philip II of Spain, at that time King of England through his marriage with Mary Tudor. Duke Thomas conformed to the new religion under Elizabeth, and not only deprived his heir of the heritage of the Faith, but placed his education partly in the hands of John Foxe, the notorious Protestant martyrologist, before sending the boy to Cambridge (St John's College).

The Duke married three times, and completed his matrimonial achievements by marrying the three heiress daughters of his third wife (the widow of Lord Dacre of Gillesland) to his own three sons. Philip's wife, Anne Dacre, was a remarkable woman, of great generosity and courage.

This distinguished couple were married at a very early age, according to the custom of the time, and Anne became a Catholic while still young.

Philip succeeded to the Earldom of Arundel in February, 1580, at the age of twenty-three, in the most brilliant period of his career. There is something extraordinarily exhilarating in the study of this magnificent personality, moving in splendour from his birth to the imperishable fame of his heroic death. Everything that the world could offer was his: rank, grace of person, intellectual gifts, a noble wife and children; everything that grace could give became his – the true Faith, a high degree of sanctity, heroic constancy under long persecution, and the crowning glory of a martyr's death.

The young Earl's first years at Court were spent in the full sunshine of the Queen's favour. He was her kinsman and premier peer of the realm, besides being a handsome, gallant youth, rich in those intellectual gifts she could appreciate so well. It is no great wonder if this period of his life will not bear too close examination; for a while he even deserted his young wife, encouraged by the Queen, who wished to keep him by her side.

Philip the courtier was the personification of sport-loving English youth. He was a great tennis player, accomplished in tilting, and fond of backgammon; he kept his own band of actors, and on several occasions he entertained the Queen with great splendour. Altogether he was the most outstanding figure in the brilliant whirl of Court life.

But Philip was destined for higher things, and in the midst of all this glittering magnificence a change came over his life. The fitful fancy of the Queen turned against him; he was a possible heir to the throne – a crime Elizabeth could brook in no man or woman – and his house had many enemies. Gradually his glory was eclipsed; suspicion and disfavour surrounded him, and his difficulties were intensified by the conversion of his young wife about this time.

Philip left the estranged Court, and returned to Arundel. There he was completely reconciled to his neglected wife, and thenceforward, to the end of his life, his whole-hearted devotion to her never wavered.

This exasperated the Queen, and very soon the young Countess was 'presented for recusancy', and sentenced to a year's imprisonment in the house of a Protestant gentleman, Sir Thomas Shirley. Thus meanly did the Queen revenge her wounded vanity, declaring her determination to 'lay her hand on Arundel's collar'.

Towards the later part of 1581 the Earl was present at Blessed Edmund Campion's famous disputes in the Tower, drawn thither possibly by mere natural curiosity to see the mysterious Jesuit whose name had become a household word in England. Probably Philip was also influenced by the fact that his own former tutor, Gregory Martin, was Campion's dearest friend.

The sight of the martyr's saintly, worn face; the body so enfeebled by the rack that he could not raise his arm, the unforgettable sound of the sweet gay voice, the whole wonderful personality of the man who charmed even his enemies, changed Philip's whole life. As he sat watching, and listening intently to the debate, his wife's constant prayer was answered; there and then the grace of conversion came to him.

Then, indeed, came a time of trial and sore temptation. For the Earl of Arundel to avow himself a Catholic would be to play into the hands of his enemies, to court ruin and probably death. He had his wife and children to consider, too, and the prospect of poverty, suffering and disgrace must have been strongly repugnant to his sunny, vital temperament.

For two years he fought against the conviction that was slowly gaining upon him, despite his struggles. The crisis came one day in 1583 as he paced up and down the

Long Gallery at Arundel Castle, wrestling desperately with the world, the flesh and the devil. At last the truth triumphed; his mind was finally made up, and he sought the first opportunity to be reconciled to the Church of his baptism. The young Countess's joy when she heard this news must have gone far to make up for the sad years of her loneliness.

But it was no easy matter for the Earl to carry out his resolution without the fact being discovered by his enemies. At first he thought of taking his family to Flanders, where they could practise their religion in peace; he sent his secretary to prepare for the journey, but the man was arrested and narrowly examined about his faith.

The Earl returned to London, and the Queen visited him at Arundel House; she requited his princely hospitality by commanding him to remain a prisoner in his own house, though there was no definite charge against him.

But Philip was not the man to be frightened by these ominous portents. On 30 September 1584, he was reconciled to the Church by Father Weston SJ and thenceforward lived the life of a most fervent Catholic. It was his proudest privilege to serve Mass, which he did frequently, and daily Mass and Communion became his greatest delight.

The Earl's freedom was restored after a while, but such a change of life as his could not escape the notice of the Court. The Queen's disfavour grew more and more marked, till at length Philip saw that the only chance of safety for himself and his family lay in flight, while flight was still possible, partly for the sake of the child whose coming they expected to crown their new-found happiness.

Philip composed a letter of explanation, to be delivered to the Queen after he had gone. In it he re-affirmed his loyalty, and set forth his reasons for leaving the country. On 14 April 1585 the Earl and Countess of Arundel left England, embarking at Littlehampton. But while the coast was still in sight, the fugitives were suddenly arrested, apparently through treachery.

The Earl was taken to the Tower of London, never to be a free man again, and never to see the little son who was born soon after. His goods were confiscated, and an enormous fine was imposed upon him; his grief for his wife and children must have been terrible, as he lay in prison, a prey to all the tortures of memory, barbed by the thought of those long years of neglect.

So he remained for three years, until, in the outburst of persecution following upon the defeat of the Armada, the Queen remembered her former favourite. He was charged with having prayed for the success of the Spanish fleet and was accused upon the evidence of an old priest, William Bennet (who was quite unnerved by the horrors of the times) of having asked for a votive Mass of the Holy Ghost for that intention. This man afterwards asked

pardon of the Earl, promising never to repeat his accusa-
tion, but he broke his promise almost immediately.

In such fashion was a trumped-up charge of treason
manufactured against the Earl; an extant letter of the
Attorney General's proves that he knew the evidence to
be false. Father Pollen SJ writes that: 'There were many
other charges brought against the Earl... in the extremely
long indictment, which bristles with charges of treason,
rebellion, murder and the like'.

Philip Howard defended himself resolutely at his trial,
all unprepared as he was, and unsupported. He denied
having prayed for the success of the Spanish fleet; and in
a letter to his wife, he wrote: 'that he was so newly made
a Catholic before his imprisonment that he knew not there
was any such Mass as of the Holy Ghost', words which
bear the very stamp of truth. As to his loyalty to the
Queen – thorny though the problem was to many simple
souls in view of her illegitimacy and excommunication –
Philip never wavered; he offered 'to serve the Queen
against all Princes, Pope and Potentate whatsoever'.

The accusers asked if he had fled the country in order
to serve the Prince of Parma; the Earl replied that 'He had
rather eat off his fingers than do anything against Her
Majesty'. The simple majesty of truth shone out from him
as he stood before the Court; his handsome youth was
withered by those years of imprisonment, but he was still
a princely figure in his 'wrought velvet gowne furred with

martins, laid about with gold lace and buttoned with gold buttons'. This was worn over 'a black satin doublett, and a payre of velvet hose', and he had a 'long high hatte upon his head, a very tall man, somewhat swarthy coloured' – doubtless because of long confinement.

Philip's defence is vividly summed up in his declaration to the public:

'For the satisfaction of all men and discharge of my conscience before God, I here protest before His Divine Majesty and all the Holy Court of Heaven, that I have committed no treason, and that the Catholic and Roman Faith, which I hold, is the only cause (so far as I can in any way imagine) why either I have been thus long imprisoned, or for which I am now ready to be executed'.

After this, his enemies, though they condemned him as guilty, dared not carry out the sentence, knowing that he would be regarded as a martyr.

A crueller fate was in store for the once brilliant young courtier. Philip was sent back to the Tower, and left in his lonely prison till he died. It was only now that the full splendour of his character showed itself. 'For eleven long and intensely painful years he kept back the weak word that would at once have brought him corporal relief. The crown for such courage must have been that of a hero.'

He was a young man still, in the prime of life, deeply in love with his wife, cruelly separated from her and their children, the youngest of whom he had never seen. Yet he lived a life of almost heroic sanctity, adding to the rigours of his prison life days of fasting, long prayers, and generous alms-giving to priests and prisoners.

Philip expected each day to be his last; his life was a constant preparation for death, and his letters to his wife reveal a perfect resignation to the Will of God. Again and again throughout those dreary years he was told that he might return to his family a free man, if he would but once attend a Protestant service, but his constancy never wavered. The inscriptions he carved on the walls of his prison during the monotonous years bear witness to his spirit:

'The more affliction we endure for Christ in this world, the more glory we shall obtain with Christ in the next. – Arundel. June 22nd, 1587.' (Anniversary of St John Fisher.)

At length, in August, 1595, he contracted a fatal illness which showed many symptoms of poison. His dying request to the Queen to let him say good-bye to his wife and the little son he had never seen was met with a last refinement of cruelty: 'If the Earl would but once go to the Protestant service, his request should not only be granted, but he should be restored to her favour, and his former estates and honours'.

Even then Philip's courage did not break down. He listened very patiently to the message, realising, perhaps, that the Queen may have meant it as a really magnanimous offer – and sent a reply characteristic of the gallant gentleman that he was. 'He declined to accept Her Majesty's favours on this condition, and that his chief sorrow was that he had but one life to lose in so good a cause.'

Philip Howard's long martyrdom came to an end, after a night of continuous prayer, at noon on Sunday, 19 October (Octave of St Wilfrid's day), 1595. He died at the early age of thirty-eight, 'in a most sweet manner, without any sign of grief or moan, only turning his head a little aside. As one falling into a pleasing sleep, he surrendered his happy soul into the hands of Almighty God, who to His so great glory had created it'.

Surely no man ever won a finer or a fitter epitaph than these last words.

The emaciated body was hurried into that obscure grave within the Tower which had received his father and grandfather. Anne, Countess of Arundel, was a worthy wife for a confessor and martyr; her widowhood was devoted to good works, the sheltering of hunted priests, and the education of her children. Her chief care was to bring up her son to walk worthily in his father's footsteps. In later years she founded the Jesuit novitiate at Ghent, and became a great benefactress to the Society, one of whose members, St Robert Southwell, was her chaplain.

Thirty years after the Earl's death, his widow was able to move his relics from their unhonoured grave. Taken first to Long Horseley, they at last found a worthy resting place in the home of his ancestors, in the FitzAlan Chapel at Arundel. There the body rests, each bone lying separate, wrapped in silk, while an inscription on the coffin gives a brief record of that splendid life which gave so great glory to the God who created it.

Saint John Jones

He was born at Clynnog Fawr near Caernarvon in 1559. He was probably already ordained when he joined the Franciscan Observants at Pontoise, France, or at Rome, in 1590. The following year he joined the 'Riformati', a reform movement within the order. After a year of intense spiritual discipline he left for England with the Blessing of Pope Clement VIII, who told him, 'Go, for I believe you are a true religious of St Francis'.

He probably worked in the London area, for we know he was once sheltered for a time i the London house of St Anne Line. Eventually, he was captured in 1597 and imprisoned in the Clink before being brought to trial in 1598. While in the Clink he was visited by many Catholics who came to see him for spiritual counselling.

John Jones was tried alongside Robert Barnes and Jane Wiseman. Against Fr Jones the charge was that he was a priest ordained abroad by authority received from the see of Rome, and the charge against the other two defendants was that they had feloniously received and comforted him.

The evidence against them was given by an informer named Nicholas Blackwell who used to run errands for Jane Wiseman. At the trial the judge allowed Barnes to make a very long defence. Barnes was able not only to disprove the evidence of Blackwell but to expose the devious and cruel methods used by the notorious Richard Topcliffe to obtain evidence against Catholics. As a result of this trial Topcliffe was largely discredited and retired shortly after to the country.

In spite of his evidence Barnes was condemned to death. Jane Wiseman refused to plead, which led automatically to the death sentence; in her case death was to be by 'pressing'. However both were later reprieved. Fr Jones, according to one account, said that he had never been guilty of any treason against the Queen or country and that he wished his case to be referred rather to the conscience of the judge than to an ignorant jury. The judge told him he was taken to be no plotter against the Queen but he was nevertheless a Romish priest who had returned to this country contrary to the statute of 1585. 'If this be a crime,' said Fr Jones, 'I must own myself guilty, for I am a priest and came to England to gain as many souls to Christ as I could'. Then he was condemned, and, falling upon his knees, he gave thanks to God in a loud voice.

On 12 July 1598 he was taken to St Thomas Waterings, Southwark (where Albany Road meets the

Old Kent Road), for execution. At the scaffold, Fr Jones declared he had never spoken a word or entertained any thought in his whole life against the Queen or his country but had daily prayed for their good. He had to wait about an hour before the execution because the hangman had forgotten to bring the rope with him. During this time Fr Jones both prayed aloud and preached to the onlookers. When the rope was delivered, he was allowed to hang until he was dead.

Saint John Rigby

Born into a family of minor gentry at Wrightington near Wigan, around 1570. His father conformed, at least outwardly, but was fully reconciled to the Catholic Church in his old age. We know little of John's early life except that he tells us himself that he conformed through weakness and fear. However for the last four or five years before his arrest he was steward to Sir Edmund Huddleston at Sawston Hall, Cambridge. The Huddlestons were a well-known Catholic family. It was Father John Gerard SJ, who was a friend of the family, who reconciled John Rigby about two years before his martyrdom.

In 1600 Mistress Fortescue, the widowed daughter of Sir Edmund, was summoned to Newgate Sessions because of her religion. She was too ill to travel and John Rigby went in her place to guarantee her good faith. He swore to the commissioners that his mistress was ill, but they then started questioning him about his own religious beliefs. He admitted he was a Catholic and refused to take the oath of allegiance. He was then tortured by being placed on a hot stone slab and having all his hair cut off. He amused the court by paying the barber three pence for his troubles. but he still would not promise to attend the Anglican service. He was then committed to Newgate prison.

The following day he appeared before Lord Justice Popham and admitted he had been reconciled to the Church by a priest, whom he named as Fr Buckley (the alias of the martyred St John Jones). He had in fact been reconciled by Fr John Gerard, but did not wish to incriminate him. To be reconciled to the Catholic Church by a priest ordained abroad was high treason under the Act of 1581, and John Rigby was sent for trial. When ordered to be placed in irons he gave the keeper sixpence for his troubles.

For the next two months he was kept at the White Lion prison in Southwark, and on 3 March 1600 he was taken to the Sessions house at Southwark, where the Lenten Assizes for Surrey were being held with Judges Francis Gawdy and George Kingsmill presiding. While the judges were having dinner, Gawdy called for Rigby because he had heard it said that he was now willing to become a good member of the established Church. Rigby replied he was a true subject of the Queen, but he was quite inflexible about non-attendance at Church. The following day he was tried for being reconciled by a Romish priest. Before the jury retired Judge Gawdy told Rigby that if he would go to Anglican service there would be no further proceedings taken. Rigby replied '... I would not wish your Lordships to think I have (as I hope) risen so many steps towards heaven, and now will wilfully let my foot slip and fall into the bottomless pit of Hell... Let your laws proceed.' He was found guilty and sentenced to be hanged, drawn and quartered. When he heard the sentence he replied, 'Deo Gratias. All is but one death My Lord.'

However, his execution was delayed and he remained in the White Lion. On 19 June he was taken to the Summer Assizes before the same two judges. Judge Kingsmill ordered him to be placed in irons and he was taken to prison and kept overnight. As he stood in court the following morning, however, the irons fell off, and when they were re-fixed they fell off again. When asked later what he thought this meant Rigby replied that he hoped it meant the severance of the bonds of his mortal life.

On 21 June he was told he was to die that very day. Between five and six in the evening he was led off to execution. Before the journey started he struck the horse that was to drag him off, saying 'Go thy way, this is the joyfullest day I ever knew'.

At the scaffold he knelt and prayed, then gave the executioner a gold coin and forgave him and all the others who had any connection with his death. He kissed the halter before it was placed round his neck, saying, 'Now do your pleasure with it'. He was cut down very quickly and landed still conscious on his feet. The executioners threw him to the ground and he was heard to say our loud 'God forgive you, Jesus receive my soul'. Then one of them put a foot over his throat and others held him down while he was dismembered. He remained conscious to the end and was able to thrust off those who held him down when they tried to pull his heart out. Then he was beheaded. The crowd going away murmured much at the great cruelty that had been used, and all kinds of people, we are told, mourned the death of St John Rigby.

Saint Anne Line

Born at Dunmow in Essex, her maiden name was Heigham. She was disinherited by her Protestant father, William Heigham, after her conversion to the Catholic faith, and her husband, Roger Line, likewise lost his inheritance on account of his religion. Arrested in 1585, he was banished from England and died in Flanders in 1594. After his death Anne, who was now left destitute, was helped by Fr John Gerard, and when he established a house for priests in London he put her in charge of it. She managed the finances, did all the housekeeping, looked after the guests, and dealt with the enquiries of strangers. Though she had poor health and suffered from many ailments, Fr Gerard tells us that she was 'full of kindness, very discreet, and possessed her soul in great peace'. On Candlemas Day 1601 the pursuivants arrived at the house during Mass. The priest escaped, but Anne was taken and later condemned to death. She was hanged at Tyburn on 27 February 1601. On the scaffold she said: 'I am sentenced for harbouring a Catholic priest, and so far am I from repenting for having done so that I wish, with all my soul, that where I have entertained one I could have entertained a thousand'.

Saint Nicholas Owen

Owen was a Jesuit Brother. He spent over twenty-five years travelling up and down England, constructing, with consummate skill, hiding places for priests. Entering the Society of Jesus about 1580, he served in succession St Edmund Campion, Fr John Gerard, and Fr Henry Garnet (Superior of the English Jesuits from 1587 to 1606). He was imprisoned twice, in 1581 and 1594, but always refused to give the authorities any information about his fellow Catholics. At the time of the Gunpowder Plot Fr Garnet and Brother Nicholas took refuge at Hinlip Hall in Worcestershire, where they were arrested soon afterwards. Nicholas was taken to the Tower of London and tortured severely to make him reveal the whereabouts of his hiding-holes, but this he resolutely refused to do. He was already a sick man, suffering from hernia, and though his persecutors took the cruel precaution of encasing him in an iron girdle to prevent rupture, the torture proved too much. His entrails burst out and he died in terrible agony in the Tower on 2 March 1606. His gaolers, to cover up their guilt, spread the story that Nicholas has committed suicide, but, as Fr Gerard wrote, 'this slander was so improbable that even his enemies did not believe it, much less his friends that were so well acquainted with his innocent life and long-continued practice in virtue'.

Saint Thomas Garnet

The protomartyr of the Jesuit College at St Omer in France (the College eventually moved to Stonyhurst in Lancashire), and nephew of Fr Henry Garnet. Born in London, he attended a grammar school at Horsham in Sussex, then went to the St Omer College and finally to the English College at Valladolid, where he was ordained priest. Returning to England in 1599, he entered the Society of Jesus in England in 1604. Not long afterwards his uncle, Fr Henry, was arrested and executed in connection with the Gunpowder Plot. Fr Thomas was arrested also at this time, imprisoned for eighteen months in the Tower of London, and then banished from England. He returned, however, the following year and was soon back again in prison. He was condemned to death for his priesthood and hanged, drawn and quartered at Tyburn on 23 June 1608. On the scaffold, in the presence of the large crowd assembled, which included many noblemen, he declared: 'I am the happiest man alive this day'.

Saint John Roberts

A native of Monmouthshire, he studied at St John's College, Oxford, and at the Inns of Court, London. Brought up a Protestant, he was reconciled to the Catholic Church in Paris, when on a visit there in 1598. From Paris he went on to the English College at Valladolid, and soon afterwards entered the Benedictine Order in that city. Ordained priest at Valladolid in 1602, the following year he returned to England and was the first Benedictine missionary to work here since the suppression of the monasteries. He laboured mostly in London, where, during the plague of 1603, he ministered to the sick and the dying with incredible zeal and made many converts. During his seven years on the mission he was arrested and imprisoned five times and banished from England on three separate occasions. His final arrest took place in London on the first Sunday of Advent in 1610, as he was saying Mass. On the scaffold, as he looked at the fire prepared for the boiling of his quarters, he cheerfully remarked: 'Here's a hot breakfast towards, despite the cold weather'. He was hanged, drawn and quartered at Tyburn on 10 December 1610.

Saint John Almond

Born at Allerton, Liverpool. He studied at the nearby grammar school at Much Woolton, then in Ireland, and finally in Rome, where he was ordained priest in 1601. He returned to England the following year and worked on the mission for the next ten years, spending some time in gaol in London about 1608. When arrested again in 1612, he refused the oath of allegiance. He declared he was ready to swear 'as much allegiance to King James as he or any Christian king could expect by the law of nature, the law of God, or the positive law of the true Church', but nothing more. He was then confined in Newgate prison until his trial nine months later, when he was condemned to death. At Tyburn, where he was hanged, drawn and quartered on 5 December 1612, he addressed the crowd, saying: 'One hour overtaketh another, and though never so long at last comes death. And yet not death, for death is the gate of life unto us, whereby we enter into everlasting blessedness'.

Saint Edmund Arrowsmith

Born at Haydock, in the parish of Winwick, in south Lancashire, in 1585. He was named Brian Arrowsmith – Edmund was the name he took in Confirmation. Both his parents and his grandparents endured much for the Catholic faith. After endeavouring in vain to go to one of the Spanish seminaries, he entered Douai and was ordained at Arras nearby. He was sent to the English mission in 1613 by the new President of the College, Dr Matthew Kellison, and worked for some ten or eleven years as a secular priest in his native Lancashire. He is said to have been 'of mean presence', ie undistinguished in his bearing, but 'of great innocency in his life, of great sincerity in his nature, of great sweetness in his conversation, and of great industry in his function', and always 'of a cheerful countenance'. But he was rather outspoken too, so that his biographer says that he 'often wished him merrily to carry salt in his pocket to season his actions, lest too much zeal without discretion might bring him too soon into danger'. In danger he soon was, for it was probably in 1622 that he was first imprisoned in Lancaster Castle and had a brief encounter with the Protestant Bishop of Chester, John Bridgeman. The Bishop was apologetic for eating meat during Lent and excused himself as being old and weak and therefore dispensed from abstinence. 'But who dispenses your lusty ministers,' snapped Arrowsmith, 'for they have no such need?'

In 1624 Arrowsmith entered the Society of Jesus, made a short noviceship of two or three months in Essex, and then returned to Lancashire, where he spent the last four years of his life as a Jesuit. It is interesting to note that his betrayal came about through a sorry marriage case. It is sometimes very easy to give offence by adhering to the Church's laws when things have gone wrong, and in such situations the example of the martyrs is an inspiration and a salutary lesson. To cause even an imaginary offence was, in the martyrs' days, the most dangerous thing possible. Lose the good will of a single member of his flock and the priest was at his or her mercy. That did not influence Arrowsmith, however, and the sad outcome was that he was betrayed by his own. After his condemnation he spent two days, awaiting execution, confined in Lancaster Castle, in a dark hole in which he could neither stand upright nor lie down, and with little or no food. Finally he was dragged out on a hurdle and received absolution in the courtyard of the castle from his fellow prisoner, St John Southworth, standing at the window of his cell. On the scaffold he was offered a pardon if he would renounce the Pope. He replied: 'Tempt me no more; I will not do it, in no case, on no condition..' He was hanged, drawn and quartered at Lancaster on 28 August 1628 in circumstances of great interest, which can be appreciated only if the story is read in full.

Saint Ambrose Barlow

His life was one of such exemplary holiness that, even if it had not been graced with martyrdom, he might still have been a candidate for canonisation. He was of the family of Barlow Hall, Manchester, and at Didsbury nearby there used to be a small font in which he is believed to have been baptised. In spite of his high birth, he was, like

Arrowsmith, unimposing in appearance, his dress, indeed, being primitive. It is fortunate that we possess contemporary sketches of both him and his father, which show family or personal characteristics and facial idiosyncrasies in such detail that they were of use in establishing that the skull preserved at Wardley Hall, Manchester, is that of the martyr.

His missionary work was mainly in the districts of Leigh, Ormskirk, Warrington and Winwick. He had the opportunity of leaving Lancashire and would probably have preserved his life had he done so. But a strange incident in his life had convinced him that it was his lot to suffer for his faith in the country and as a result he could not be prevailed upon to leave it. In 1628 he was able to be of service by ministering to Fr Arrowsmith, then in captivity in Lancaster gaol. On the night of Arrowsmith's execution that martyr seemingly appeared to Barlow in southern Lancashire and told him that he would be next to suffer at Lancaster, then three other priests after him, and after these no more. This was duly recorded before any opportunity arose to check up on its fulfilment. Now the little manuscript notebook in the writer's possession, to which we have already referred, enlarges on this most interestingly. It reads: 'In the morning Mr Barlow told the family what had happened to him in the night and said: "Had the apparition been a night later, I should have judged it a real one; but as it is, I suspect it was an illusion, because this day (Friday) is the usual execution day." But upon certain information that Mr Arrowsmith was executed the day before [in margin: viz. Thursday, the 28th of August, 1628], Mr Barlow was convinced of the truth of what he had seen and heard: so that (some years after) when the house was set about by those that came to take him, he bid the family open the door and let them in, because he was satisfied it was the will of God he should follow Mr Arrowsmith in dying for his faith.' Barlow was thus not over-credulous about the reality of the appearance, and he only believed in it when he learned that Arrowsmith's execution had taken place a day earlier than expected, ie *before* his vision.

Whatever happened in fact, events came to pass as predicted and again the manuscript notebook records a strange fact about the fulfilment. Barlow's execution, in 1641, was indeed the next martyrdom to follow at Lancaster, and a triple execution took place there in 1646, and then no more. But in the ordinary course of events there should have been more, for three other priests were later condemned at Lancaster in the time of the Oates' Plot – Fathers John Penketh SJ, Richard Barton and Richard Birkett. But they were never executed, the two former being freed, while Birkett died in prison. What is more, the Lancashire Catholics never expected them to be executed for, even after the sentence, such reliance was placed upon Arrowsmith's prediction that they assured themselves that the priests would not be put to death.

Sentence on Barlow, at any rate, was duly carried out and his head and quarters were impaled upon the Collegiate Church at Manchester and on the walls of Lancaster Castle.

Saint Alban Roe

Born in Suffolk and brought up a Protestant. While a student at the University of Cambridge, he became a Catholic, and then went to Douai to study for the priesthood. He entered the Benedictine Order at Dieulouard in France in 1612, was ordained priest, and then returned to England. He was soon captured and imprisoned, and was banished from England in 1623, but shortly afterwards he returned. About two years later he was again arrested and spent the remainder of his life, about seventeen years, in confinement, mostly in the Fleet prison in London. His gaiety and holiness soon won the hearts of his gaolers and he was allowed not only to receive visitors but to go out on parole, and thus he was able to carry on his priestly ministry. In spite of frequent bouts of severe pain caused by 'the stone', he was well known for his good humour and was always ready for a laugh or joke or game of cards with his fellow prisoners. At the beginning of 1642 he was finally brought to trial for his priesthood and hanged, drawn and quartered at Tyburn on 31 January.

St Henry Morse

One of the most interesting of the Northern martyrs as he was arrested four times, banished thrice and then, after his fourth and final arrest, executed. He was born at Brome on the borders of Norfolk and Suffolk in 1595. His parents had conformed to the new State religion and he was brought up as a Protestant. His original intention was to become a lawyer. In the course of his studies, he became convinced of the truth of the Catholic faith and went abroad to be reconciled. He decided to become a priest and returned to England to settle his affairs. On his return he was offered the Oath of Supremacy which he refused to take and for his refusal he was thrown into prison. Here he remained for four years. On his release and subsequent banishment, he went first to the college at Douai and then to Rome where he was ordained in 1624. After his ordination, he joined the Society of Jesus.

His first missionary appointment in England was as chaplain to that heroic Catholic lady, Dorothy Lawson of St Anthony's, near Newcastle, where he remained for one year. His superiors then decided that he should go abroad again to finish his novitiate in the Society of Jesus. Government spies were on the watch. As the ship on which he was to travel abroad was leaving the Tyne, it was boarded by officials and Henry Morse was arrested on suspicion of being a priest. He was thrown into the Newgate prison in Newcastle and then transferred to

York where he remained a prisoner for four years. He was then released and banished for a second time. In 1633 he was back again in England, this time in London, where for a year he looked after the plague-stricken Catholics of that city. He was arrested once again, imprisoned, condemned, granted a royal pardon and banished for a third time. Nothing seemed to deter him and we find him back again in this country, this time in the North. He was arrested while on a sick call on the Cumberland-Durham border. He was taken to Durham and eventually shipped to London where he again stood trial on 17 January 1645. This time the sentence of death was carried out on 1 February of that same year. His last words were. 'I pray that my death may be some atonement for the sins of this Kingdom'.

Saint John Southworth

He was born in Lancashire in 1592 and studied at Douai, where he was ordained priest in 1619, and then returned to his native country as a missionary. Arrested in 1627, he was condemned to death for his priesthood, but was reprieved and in 1630 banished from England. He was soon back again, and in the years 1635–36 he worked with St Henry Morse amongst the plague-stricken in London. He suffered three further periods of imprisonment before his final arrest in 1654, when he was again condemned to death for his priesthood. This time the sentence was carried out and he was hanged, drawn and quartered at Tyburn on 28 June in that year. On the scaffold he addressed the huge crowd that had gathered in spite of the rain. 'My faith is my crime,' he told them, 'the performance of my duty the occasion of my condemnation'. His body was found buried at Douai in 1927 and is now venerated in Westminster Cathedral, London.

Saint John Plessington

He was born at Dimples Hall, near Garstang, Lancashire. He studied at a Jesuit school at Scarisbrick Hall near Ormskirk, at St Omer, and at Valladolid. Ordained priest at Segovia in 1662, he returned to England the following year and worked first at Holywell in Flintshire – where St Winefride's well was famous as a place of pilgrimage – and then at Puddington Hall in Cheshire. He was eventually arrested in 1679, in the wave of persecution that followed the Titus Oates Plot, and condemned for his priesthood. He was hanged, drawn and quartered on Barrel Well Hill, Chester, on 19 July in that year.

Saint Philip Evans and Saint John Lloyd

They were martyred together outside Cardiff Castle on 22 July 1679. Philip Evans was born at Monmouth in 1645 and studied at St Omer, where he entered the Society of Jesus in 1665. He was ordained priest at Liege ten years later, and then returned home and worked as a missionary in south Wales. At the time of the Titus Oates persecution he refused to hide, even though a local Justice of the Peace had offered a reward of £200 for his apprehension. He was captured at Sker in Glamorganshire in December 1678 and spent five months in gaol in Cardiff Castle, where he shared a cell with St John Lloyd.

John Lloyd was born in Brecknockshire and studied at Ghent and Valladolid, where he was ordained priest in 1653. He then returned to Wales and laboured on the mission there for twenty-four years. Like Philip Evans, he was a victim of the Titus Oates persecution. He was arrested at Lenllyn in Glamorganshire in November 1678 and imprisoned in Cardiff Castle. Several men were flogged for refusing to give evidence against the two priests, but eventually an old woman and her daughter were persuaded to testify that they had seen them say Mass. Philip Evans was executed first, and hence John Lloyd had the additional ordeal of seeing his fellow priest hanged, drawn and quartered before undergoing the same barbarous fate himself.

Saint John Wall

He came of a Norfolk family and was born in 1620, in Lancashire (where precisely we do not know; there is no evidence to connect him with Chingle Hall, near Preston, which belonged to a Lancashire family of the same name). He studied at Douai and Rome, where he was ordained priest in 1645. He returned to England in 1648, then joined the Franciscan Order at Douai in 1651. Four years later he came back again to England and worked in Worcestershire and the adjoining counties for over twenty years. He was finally arrested at Rushock Court in Worcestershire in 1678 and, in spite of his spirited defence at his trial at Worcester Assizes, was condemned for his priesthood. His execution was postponed while he was sent to London to be questioned by Titus Oates and his associate, William Bedloe, but they failed to implicate him in the alleged plot. He was hanged, drawn and quartered at Worcester on 22 August 1679.

Saint John Kemble

Kemble was born at St Weonards, Herefordshire, about 1600. He studied at Douai and was ordained priest there in 1625. Returning home, he worked in Herefordshire and Monmouthshire, with his headquarters at Pembridge Castle in the former county, for more than fifty years. But eventually he too fell a victim to the Titus Oates scare. Arrested in November 1678, he was condemned as a priest at the Assizes at Hereford the following March. Like St John Wall, he was then sent to London, with St David Lewis, to be examined by Titus Oates and others, and finally brought back to Hereford for his execution. On 22 August 1679, when he was eighty years old, the news came to him in prison that he was to die that day.

He asked for time to say his prayers, smoke his last pipe and drink a cup of sack. On the scaffold, seeing the executioner hesitate, he said, 'Be not afraid, do thy office. I forgive thee with all my heart. Thou wilt do me a greater kindness than discourtesy.' But the executioner was clumsy and Fr Kemble hung for half an our before he died. No one had the heart to cut down the saintly old man, so they carried out the revolting sentence of drawing and quartering only after he was dead.

Saint David Lewis

Born at Abergavenny, Monmouthshire, in 1616. Brought up a Protestant, at the age of sixteen he was reconciled to the Catholic Church while visiting Paris. he then studied at Rome, where he was ordained priest in 1642 and entered the Society of Jesus in 1645. Two years later he returned home and worked in south Wales for over thirty years. His headquarters was the Cwm, a hamlet in Herefordshire where the Jesuits occupied two remote farmhouses, well known as a shelter for hunted priests. Eventually he was arrested in November 1678, at Llantarnan in Monmouthshire, and condemned for his priesthood at the Assizes in Monmouth the following March. Then, as mentioned, he was taken to London with St John Kemble, to be examined by Titus Oates, and finally brought back to Usk in Monmouthshire, where he was hanged, drawn and quartered on 27 August 1679.